Try It [barcode: D0635136] Charlie Brown

Charles M. Schulz

Selected Cartoons from
You're Something Else, Charlie Brown, Vol. 2

CORONET BOOKS
Hodder Fawcett Ltd., London

Copyright © 1967 by
United Feature Syndicate, Inc.
First published 1974 by Fawcett
Publications Inc., New York
Coronet edition 1974

Printed and bound in Great Britain for
Coronet Books,
Hodder Fawcett Ltd,
St. Paul's House, Warwick Lane,
London, EC4P 4AH
by Hazell Watson & Viney Ltd,
Aylesbury, Bucks

ISBN 0 340 18831 6

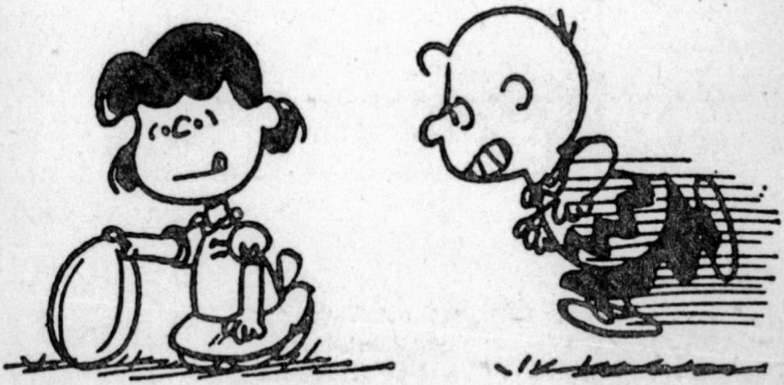

NO AFTER-DINNER SPEAKER?

I REFUSE TO LET A STUPID CHAIN LETTER DOMINATE MY LIFE!
I'M GOING TO DEFY BAD LUCK! I'M GOING TO RIP THIS LETTER TO SHREDS, AND NEVER ANSWER IT!
I'M FREE!!

➤

ON HALLOWEEN NIGHT THE "GREAT PUMPKIN" RISES OUT OF THE PUMPKIN PATCH THAT HE PICKS AS THE MOST SINCERE

THEN HE FLIES THROUGH THE AIR BRINGING TOYS TO ALL THE GOOD CHILDREN IN THE WORLD!

JUST THINK, SNOOPY, IF HE PICKS THIS PUMPKIN PATCH, YOU AND I WILL BE HERE TO SEE HIM!

FRANKLY, THIS LOOKS LIKE A GOOD PLACE TO GET MUGGED!

BEAUTIFUL, ISN'T IT?

YES, BUT SOMETHING SEEMS STRANGE...

HI, PAL..WELCOME TO MY TEAM...LET ME FILL YOU IN ON A FEW THINGS...
I'M A GREAT BELIEVER IN WINTER CONDITIONING! EVERY DAY BETWEEN NOW AND NEXT SPRING, IT'S GOING TO BE RUN, RUN, RUN, RUN...
SO LET'S GET GOING!
I DON'T KNOW...HE MAY BE A GOOD PLAYER, AND I'M GLAD I HAVE HIM ON MY TEAM, BUT I STILL SAY HE'S THE FUNNIEST LOOKING KID I'VE EVER SEEN!
SCHULZ

Peanuts
CHARLES M. SCHULZ

All these books are available at your bookshop or newsagent, or can be ordered direct from the publisher. Just tick the titles you want and fill in the form below.

....

CORONET BOOKS, P.O. Box 11, Falmouth, Cornwall.
Please send cheque or postal order. No currency, and allow the following for postage and packing:
1 book—10p, 2 books—15p, 3 books—20p, 4–5 books—25p, 6–9 books— 4p per copy, 10–15 books—2½p per copy, over 30 books free within the U.K.
Overseas—please allow 10p for the first book and 5p per copy for each additional book.

Name..

Address..

....